MW01104303

ECONOMY AND INDUSTRY IN ANCIENT GREECE

MELANIE ANN APEL

The Rosen Publishing Group's
PowerKids Press™
PRIMARY SOURCE

New York

To precious Hayden, calling "Mama" from your crib. I love you, baby!

Published in 2004 by The Rosen Publishing Group, Inc.
29 East 21st Street, New York, NY 10010

First Edition

Editor: Joanne Randolph
Book Design: Michael DeGuzman
Layout Design: Kim Sonsky
Photo Researcher: Peter Tomlinson

Photo Credits: Cover (center), p. 20 (inset) © Gianni Dagli Orti/CORBIS; cover (right), pp. 7 (top and center), 8, 16 (top) Erich Lessing/Art Resource, NY; p. 4 British Museum, London, U.K./Bridgeman Art Library; p. 4 (inset) © Mark Oatman/Getty Images; p. 7 (bottom) The Art Archive/Musée du Louvre Paris/Dagli Orti; p. 8 (inset) The Art Archive/British Museum/Eileen Tweedy; pp. 11, 12, 15 (bottom) Ashmolean Museum, Oxford, U.K./Bridgeman Art Library; p. 15 (top) Musée du Louvre, Paris/Bridgeman Art Library; p. 16 (bottom) Galleria de Museo Estense, Modena, Italy/Bridgeman Art Library; p. 19 The Art Archive/Dagli Orti; p. 19 (inset) The Art Archive/Agora Museum Athens/Dagli Orti; p. 20 The Art Archive/National Archaeological Museum Athens/Dagli Orti.

Library of Congress Cataloging-in-Publication Data

Apel, Melanie Ann.
  Economy and industry in ancient Greece / Melanie Ann Apel.
     v. cm. — (Primary sources of ancient civilizations. Greece)
Includes bibliographical references and index.
Contents: Farming and agriculture—Mining—Currency—Work to be done—Manufacturing pottery—The importance of pottery—Precious oils and cosmetics—Shopping at the marketplace—Foreign and domestic trade—Ships.
  ISBN 0-8239-6774-3 — ISBN 0-8239-8942-9 (paperback)
  1. Greece—Economic conditions—To 146 B.C.—Juvenile literature. [1. Greece—Economic conditions—To 146 B.C. 2. Industries—Greece—History.] I. Title. II. Series.
  HC37 .A63 2004
  330.938—dc21   2003002333
Manufactured in the United States of America

Contents

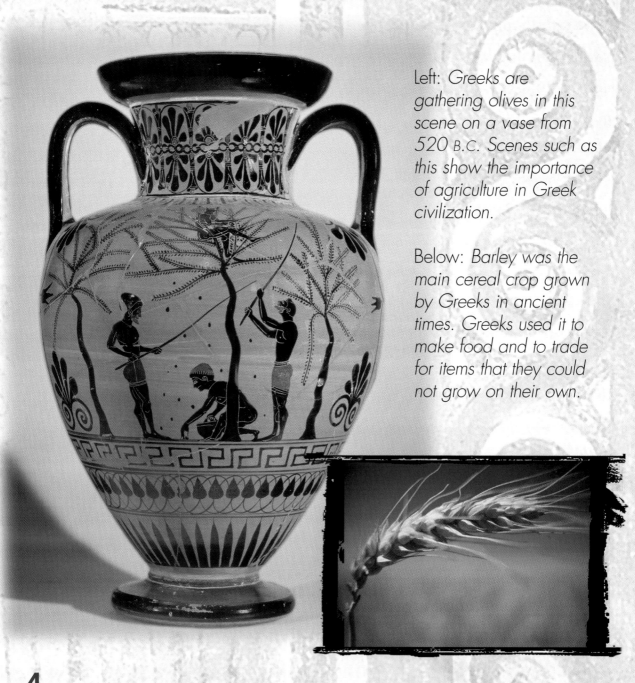

Left: *Greeks are gathering olives in this scene on a vase from 520 B.C. Scenes such as this show the importance of agriculture in Greek civilization.*

Below: *Barley was the main cereal crop grown by Greeks in ancient times. Greeks used it to make food and to trade for items that they could not grow on their own.*

Farming and Agriculture

The economy of ancient Greece depended heavily on its agriculture. In fact, 90 percent of the men in Greece were farmers. Unfortunately, the soil was rocky and of poor quality, and there was little rain during the year. Barley and wheat were important crops. Many farmers found that barley needed less water to grow than did wheat. Because there was little water, barley became the main cereal crop of ancient Greece. Olives and grapes grew well in the land, too. Greeks cooked with olives and pressed them to make olive oil. They used grapes to make wine. Olives and grapes also served as a base to make perfumes and soaps. These were the best crops to sell at the market to make money for the family.

Mining

Mining was one of the main industries in ancient Greece. Different city-states were known for different metals. Supplies of gold and silver were mined in Thrace's mountains and on the island of Sífnos. Mainland Greece and the Aegean Islands provided iron ore. Cyprus was known for copper. Athens had supplies of silver and lead ore. To get to these precious metals, the Greeks had to mine. Miners worked in tight spaces, with little light or fresh air. They used hammers, picks, and chisels to get at the ore. Then the ore had to be carried up to the surface in sacks or baskets. Special craftspeople, such as blacksmiths and metalsmiths, shaped metals into useful items. The items were valuable in trade. Around the seventh century B.C., ore was also made into coins.

The ruins of the silver-washing plant at the silver mines in Laurion, Greece, are shown above. The precious metals sank and were held in the holes shown. After the silver ore (top right) was mined, it was used to make items such as this silver cup (bottom right).

8

Currency

Before the ancient Greeks had money, they used a system called bartering. In the 700s B.C., people began to use coins as currency in addition to the barter system. The first coins were called drachmas. Drachmas were made of silver. Other Greek coins were made of electrum, a mix of silver and gold. Coins from foreign, or faraway, lands were used in ancient Greek trade, also. For example, the Persians used a pure gold coin called a *daric*. Gold coins were also used in Egypt. In Greece, coins were made by hand in workshops called mints. To make the coins, a piece of metal was placed on an anvil between two molds. A worker hammered the molds, which shaped the metal.

◄ *Each city-state stamped its coins with a picture. Athens stamped this silver coin with an owl. The owl was the bird of Athena, the goddess of Athens.* Inset: *The Persian daric was stamped with a bowman.*

Work to Be Done

Many Greeks were skilled laborers, called artisans. A man usually learned his craft from his father, beginning at an early age. Knowledge of work such as carpentry, leatherworking, and sculpting were passed down through a system of apprenticeship. The hardest crafts were pottery and metalworking, both of which required great attention to detail. Artisans were responsible for making the everyday items people used, such as dishes. Weavers created cloth that could be made into clothing or other items. Each item had to be made individually and took many steps to complete. Men who did not learn a trade often worked in construction. As ancient Greek civilization grew, there were many temples, homes, forts, and theaters to be built.

Above: *This piece of pottery shows a young craftsman making a helmet.*

Right: *This vase shows shoemakers making shoes.*

11

Manufacturing Pottery

People in the ancient world made by hand everything they needed. Different parts of Greece were known for the things they manufactured. At Kerameikos, in the northwest corner of Athens, artisans made all sorts of ceramic goods, including roof tiles, figurines, large sculptures, architectural decorations, and pottery. Made of clay, pots were made on a potter's wheel turned by the potter's feet. Potters dried the clay pots in kilns, or special ovens. They created the few different colors seen in Greek pottery by controlling the oxygen flow to the pot. Air around the pot that was high in oxygen produced the color red. To get gray and black, the amount of fresh air had to be reduced.

◀ *This is an example of black-figure pottery, made in Athens. In black-figure pottery the image was made in black on the natural red background of the clay.*

The Importance of Pottery

Pottery provided another large industry for the ancient Greeks. Ancient Greek pottery has been found all over the world. This shows how well the ancient Greek system of trade worked. Thousands of ancient Greek vases have been found buried in tombs in the graveyards of central and northern Etruria, in Italy. Although the Etruscans had a great deal of ancient Greek pottery, very few examples of Etruscan-manufactured goods have been found in Greece. This leads archaeologists to believe that the ancient Greeks traded pottery for iron, lead, and bronze.

Top: *This container was made in the Corinthian style. The Greek city-state of Corinth controlled the trade of pottery until* ▶ *around the middle of the sixth century* B.C.

This container for cosmetics or small items was created in the fifth century B.C., in Athens. Around 525 B.C., the city-state of Athens became the most successful in the pottery trade. The pottery that came from Athens was popular because of its high quality.

Large amounts of perfumes and scented oils were stored in a large container called a pelike. Once these perfumes and oils reached where they were going, they were poured into smaller, fancier, and usually hand-carved bottles, such as these red-figure alabastrons.

Precious Oils and Cosmetics

The creating and selling of perfumes and cosmetics, or makeup, was an important industry in ancient Greece. Ancient Greek women used perfumes, oils, and cosmetics such as skin glosses, eyeshadow, and paints. Some even used hair dye. Greeks traded these goods throughout the Mediterranean region. Around the eighth century B.C., perfume and makeup containers from Corinth, Rhodes, and eastern Greece could be found in many places overseas. The cosmetics were stored in hand-carved containers made from the shells of Red Sea *Tridacna*, a kind of clam. Hundreds of years later, Athenian beauty products became popular and precious oils were poured into containers called *lekythoi* for safe shipment.

Top: *This cup shows women with flowers and perfume bottles. The Greeks used flowers to give perfume its pleasant scent.*

Shopping at the Marketplace

The marketplaces of ancient Greece were called agoras. The agora was an open-air market surrounded by many beautiful buildings. Greeks shopped in different areas of the large, busy marketplace for goods such as fish, pottery, bronze bowls, oils, perfumes, cloth, and various regional foods. Officials carefully watched trade in the agora. For example, *metronomoi* made certain that traders used the correct weights and measures and that the traders were giving people a fair deal. To check a trader's weights, metronomoi compared them to a standard set of weights. *Agoranomoi* were in charge of checking the traders' goods to make sure they were of high quality.

The Greeks visited the agora to buy or sell goods. Inset: lead weights, such as these, were used to make sure that everyone paid a fair price for products. ▶

19

Foreign and Domestic Trade

Greece is a peninsula and a group of small islands. People on these islands had different products and natural resources to trade with each other. The ancient Greeks also traded their resources, such as olive oil and wine, with neighboring civilizations on the Mediterranean Sea, such as Syria and Egypt. They imported grain from cities on the coast of the Black Sea. They traded for incense from Syria, beef from Italy, rope and sails from Egypt, leather from North Africa, and cushions and rugs from Carthage. Because of this trade, goods manufactured in Greece could be found as far away as North Africa, Spain, the Balkans, and India by 300 B.C.

◀ *Because most Greeks lived on the coasts of the Mediterranean and Black Seas, they relied on fish for food. Inset: They traded fish for other goods, such as this piece of jewelry from Egypt.*

Ships

All the trade done in ancient Greece made a large shipbuilding industry necessary. The ancient Greeks used several different types of ships. One of these was the cargo ship. Sailors used cargo ships to pick up and drop off trade goods. Shipbuilders also built a ship called the trireme, which was a long wooden battleship. The Greeks used these ships to protect their coasts as well as to attack and conquer neighboring lands. Ships made it possible for the Greek economy to flourish, or do well. Artifacts from Greek expansion can be found across Europe and in lands such as Turkey and Egypt. The beautiful objects created by the ancient Greek industries tell us a lot about what life was like in this ancient civilization.

Glossary

agriculture (A-grih-kul-cher) The science of producing crops and raising livestock, or animals.

anvil (AN-vul) A large object on which metal is hammered into shape.

apprenticeship (uh-PREN-tis-ship) A period in which a young person works with an experienced person to learn a skill or trade.

archaeologists (ar-kee-AH-luh-jists) People who study the remains of peoples to understand how they lived.

architectural (ar-kih-TEK-chuh-rul) Having to do with the style and the creation of buildings.

artifacts (AR-tih-fakts) Objects created and produced by humans.

bartering (BAR-tur-ing) Trading.

ceramic (suh-RAH-mik) Made from matter, such as clay, that is heated until it hardens.

chisels (CHIH-zulz) Sharp, metal tools used to cut wood or stone.

city-states (SIH-tee-stayts) Independent states made up of a city and its surrounding areas.

economy (ih-KAH-nuh-mee) The way a country or a business manages its resources.

expansion (ek-SPAN-shun) The widening or opening of an area.

incense (IN-sents) Spice or scent that is burned.

kilns (KILNZ) Ovens used to burn, to bake, or to dry something.

natural resources (NA-chuh-rul REE-sors-ez) Things in nature that can be used by people.

ore (OR) A rock that contains metal.

peninsula (peh-NIN-suh-luh) Land surrounded by water on three sides.

Index

A
Aegean Islands, 6
agora(s), 18
agriculture, 5
artisans, 10
Athens, 13

B
bartering, 9

C
clothing, 10
coins, 6, 9
construction, 10
crops, 5

F
farmers, 5

M
market, 5, 18

metals, 6
miners, 6
mints, 9

P
perfumes, 5, 17–18
pots, 13
pottery, 13–14

R
resources, 21

S
sailors, 22
Sifnos, 6
soil, 5

T
trade, 6, 18,
      21–22
trireme, 22

Primary Sources

Cover: Ships at sea with dolphins. Sixteenth century B.C. **Inset and Page 8.** Athenian silver tetra drachma with owl on the reverse side. Fourth century B.C. Kunsthistorisches Museum. Vienna, Austria. **Page 4.** Olive gathering. Athenian black-figure amphora. Greek School. Circa 520 B.C. British Museum. London, United Kingdom. **Page 7. Top.** Ancient silver mines in Laurion, Greece. Silver washing plant, close-up of center channel. The precious metals sank and were retained in the cups. Sixth century B.C. **Center.** Pure silver produced at the ancient silver mines. Sifnos, Greece. **Bottom.** Cup. Silver with gold appliqué. Eighth to seventh century B.C. Kamiros, Rhodes, Greece. Musée du Louvre. Paris, France. **Page 8. Inset.** Persian gold coin. **Page 11. Top.** Attic red-figure cup decorated with a scene of a young helmet-maker. Antiphon Painter. Circa 480 B.C. Ashmolean Museum. Oxford, United Kingdom. **Bottom.** Detail of an Attic black-figure pelike decorated with a scene of a shoemaker cutting leather. Eucharides painter. Circa 500–475 B.C. Ashmolean Museum. Oxford, United Kingdom. **Page 12.** Attic black-figure stamnos decorated with a scene of boxers at a banquet. Michigan Painter. Circa 520–500 B.C. Ashmolean Museum. Oxford, United Kingdom. **Page 15. Top.** Detail of a krater with a scene of a funeral banquet. Corinthian style. Late seventh to early sixth century B.C. Musée du Louvre. Paris, France. **Bottom.** Attic red-figure pyxis (container for cosmetics or trinkets) with a scene showing women and cupids. Fifth century B.C. Ashmolean Museum. Oxford, United Kingdom. **Page 16. Top.** Women with flowers and perfume bottles. Red-figure cup. Fifth century B.C. Musée Vivenel. Compiegne, France. **Bottom.** Red-figure alabastrons, one with a female figure seated on a rock. Galleria e Museo Estense. Modena, Italy. **Page 19. Inset.** Lead weights. Classical Greek. Found in the agora. Athens, Greece. The Agora Museum. Athens. **Page 20. Left.** Egyptian Twenty-First Dynasty Pectoral with Scarab Circa 1069–945 B.C. **Right.** Fisherman. Painted terra-cotta vase. Cycladic period (3200–2000 B.C.). Phylacopi, Greece. National Archaeological Museum. Athens, Greece.

Web Sites

Due to the changing nature of Internet links, PowerKids Press has developed an online list of Web sites related to the subject of this book. This site is updated regularly. Please use this link to access the list:
www.powerkidslinks.com/psaciv/econgre/